Praise for Leadership Chaos to Clarity

"People are every organization's greatest asset to compete in today's business environment. *Leadership Chaos to Clarity* will help any team focus their energy in the right areas to achieve their goals."

—**DAVID MATTSON,** President and CEO, Sandler

"Tim has used his years of experience as a leader to provide the reader with real strategies and skills to build a highly effective team and organization."

—**WAYNE MILNER,** Chief Operating Officer, Washington Athletic Club

"I have witnessed Tim use the *Leadership Chaos to Clarity* strategies first-hand to lead and develop a team and organization. If fully committed to the process, excellent things can and will happen. The LCP closes the loop on industry best practices to create and foster an environment of constant improvement."

—**DAN FISS,** Sr. Corporate F&B Director, Invited

"I have collaborated with Tim Rowe and marveled at his deep knowledge and passion for inspiring great leadership. His new book, *Leadership Chaos to Clarity,* delivers on his fervent desire to help organizations succeed through an insightful model that Tim has developed and has proven to work!"

—**KELLY ELBIN,** 30-year golf industry veteran

"Tim Rowe presents his Leadership Clarity Pyramid in a straightforward and compelling manner. Any manager or leader seeking to embrace a framework that will move her or his team or company forward should study this work. It WILL make a difference."

—**RAY CRONIN,** Founder, Club Benchmarking

"Tim has been a tremendous mentor and friend. His leadership and guidance have been an inspiration and pivotal in my career. *Leadership Chaos to Clarity* will be the blueprint I use to coach and develop my team."

—**DALE DAVIS,** PGA, Director of Golf, Firestone Country Club

LEADERSHIP
CHAOS
TO
CLARITY

LEADERSHIP CHAOS TO CLARITY

Five Strategic Steps Great Leaders Take to Unlock Their Company's Potential

TIM ROWE

NAPLES, FL

Copyright © 2023 by Tim Rowe

All rights reserved.

Published in the United States by
O'Leary Publishing
www.olearypublishing.com

The views, information, or opinions expressed in this book are solely those of the authors involved and do not necessarily represent those of O'Leary Publishing, LLC.

The author has made every effort possible to ensure the accuracy of the information presented in this book. However, the information herein is sold without warranty, either expressed or implied. Neither the author, publisher nor any dealer or distributor of this book will be held liable for any damages caused either directly or indirectly by the instructions or information contained in this book. You are encouraged to seek professional advice before taking any action mentioned herein.

All rights reserved. No part of this book may be reproduced or transmitted in any form by any means, electronic, mechanical, photocopy, recording, or other without the prior and express written permission except for brief cited quotes.

For information on getting permission for reprints and excerpts, contact O'Leary Publishing at admin@olearypublishing.com.

ISBN: 978-1-952491-47-4 (print)
ISBN: 978-1-952491-48-1 (ebook)
Library of Congress Control Number: 2022921527

Editing by Heather Davis Desrocher
Proofreading Kat Langenheim
Cover and interior design by Jessica Angerstein

Printed in the United States of America

For Amanda, Emerson, Teagan and Everett,

and,

Servant leaders everywhere who work
to create an environment for their teams
to become incredibly successful.

CONTENTS

Preface i

Introduction - The Leadership Clarity Pyramid 1

PART I - THE TOOLS

Chapter 1 - Vision 9

Chapter 2 - Values 21

Chapter 3 - Strategy 31

Chapter 4 - Dynamic Operating Systems 43

Chapter 5 - Goals 55

PART II - APPLICATION

Chapter 6 - Create Clarity 65

Chapter 7 - Apply the Tools, Phase 1 Leadership 71

Chapter 8 - Apply the Tools, Phase 2 The Team 89

Chapter 9 - Dynamic System Implementation 111

Chapter 10 - Success 123

Acknowledgments 131

About the Author 133

Preface

Far too many really smart people in leadership positions sacrifice their well-being in an effort to make great things happen for their companies – and yet, are still not delivering the required results. I have been there too.

If this is where you are, I invite you to stop. Just stop. Stop working too many hours. Stop experiencing tremendously unhealthy levels of stress. Stop letting your business run you. Sacrificing your well-being is not the answer – there is a better way.

Sure, when you first begin any leadership position worth having, your stress meter is going to run high – potentially very high. Yes, initially you will work a lot of hours. However, if that stress meter and those hours do not start trending down soon, you are doing something wrong. *Leadership Chaos to Clarity* is here to guide you through that better way.

Successful organizational leadership requires that you pivot from working harder, to compelling others to focus *their* energy on using the best possible strategies to achieve clearly defined goals. When that magic happens consistently – when your whole team is vigorously and efficiently working together toward clearly-defined, common goals – you will deliver amazing results – and provide a work and life balance to you and your team that only the best leaders can deliver.

So how do you make this "magic" happen? You inspire and galvanize your team's efforts and attitudes by using the best tools available to eliminate leadership chaos and create clarity.

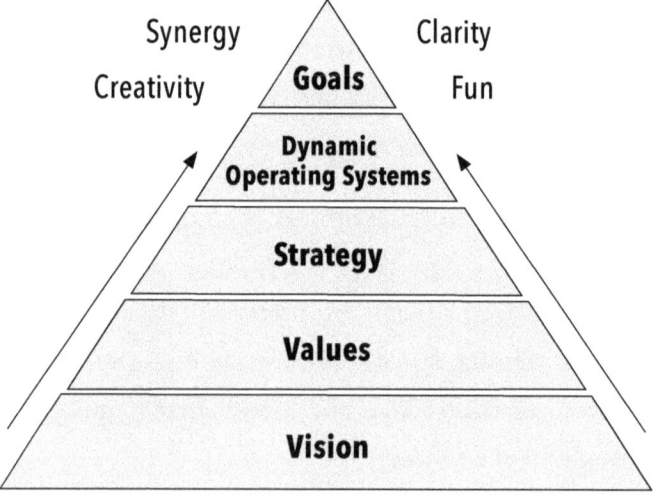

This **Leadership Clarity Pyramid** (**LCP**) is just such a tool. Its use is sequential, from the bottom of the pyramid to the top, and it will help you create your dream company. It is meant to be used at all levels of an organization – optimally starting at the top. The end-result of its use will be a rock solid foundation upon which your team's efforts can confidently stand. Your entire team will clearly know where the company is going, what is important, and how it will deliver the necessary performance.

As the leader, you will create a diverse team of people led by clear systems of operation that accomplish more than you or they ever thought possible. Perhaps most importantly, that includes achieving lasting and meaningful work and life experiences. While the work may be intense, if you require everyone's creative and synergistic best efforts to overcome the challenges, you will accomplish much, have fun, and truly appreciate the deep, trusting relationships that will form.

This book is made up of two parts. Part I describes the tools, including the **LCP** that will radically improve your ability to create clarity. Part II describes how to apply those tools. Whether your company has two team members or two thousand, implementing the clarity-generating strategy in Part II, will positively affect team-member performance and satisfaction. Those improvements will then deliver material results in the form of enhanced delivery of your company's key performance indicators.

I have had both successes and failures in my more than 40 years of leadership experience. Those experiences have come in various industries – most notably: hospitality, wellness, private club operations, and resort development. For the last 16 years, I have been teaching the use of the **LCP** to both my team and others. The results have been so consistently outstanding that I knew I needed to create this book to reach more leaders who want to be their best.

In the pages that follow, I will share detailed descriptions of what each step entails, and how it will improve your success as a leader and, by extension, your company's success. If you plan to use this process to transform your operation, I highly recommend that before starting you read the entire book to understand the process as a whole. As you read, make notes in the margins, or highlight sections or tools that are particularly relevant to your situation. Also, before you begin the **LCP** process, be sure to use some type of project management system, or chart, to map out a timeline for the entire effort. Your ability to deliver results against your timeline will be an important signal to your team that you have what it takes to lead.

I am pleased that you are adding the **LCP** tools to your leadership tool box. Their use will dramatically improve your ability to create clarity, thereby reducing chaos. The result will be a systems-driven and laser-focused workforce that enjoys the highest-possible levels of employee satisfaction while achieving the visionary and financial goals for your company.

Let's dive in!

Introduction

Make no mistake – your people are hungry for clarity – clarity of vision – clarity of standards and expectations – clarity of communication – clarity of purpose. Great leaders know that if they can create and nurture clarity for their team members, they will earn their trust, inspire loyalty and lower turnover. In addition, leaders who create clarity unlock the potential of team members to, quite literally, achieve levels of performance for themselves and the organization that would never have been thought possible before.

The best way that I have found to create clarity is to use the **Leadership Clarity Pyramid (LCP)**. Let's start by taking a brief look at each of the steps of this powerful tool.

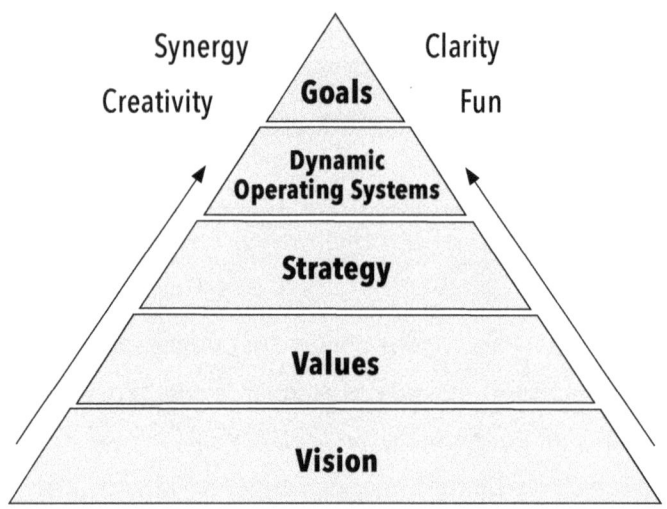

Vision

Great leaders have a clear vision of what their company or department should *look* and *feel* like when it is operating effectively and achieving its goals. They see it in their mind's eye and can describe its unique characteristics. If the operation is customer-facing, successful leaders can see from the customer's perspective. If it is a back-of-the-house operation, they can see the effectiveness of the operation from the perspective of both the team members and the company. When they observe the current operations, they know if what they *see* and *feel* is congruent with their ideal vision.

Values

Great leaders identify core values that act as guideposts to create systems and manage their companies. Employees, customers, investors, and the community want to know what your company stands for, and your core values enable you to tell them. Great leaders use these core values to guide decision-making.

Strategy

Great leaders invest the necessary time creating and thoroughly analyzing the strategies they will use to both deliver their unique operational vision, and achieve consistent delivery of the enterprise's measurable goals. Before memorializing strategies as dynamic operating systems, they are tested to determine if they can deliver the minimum financial results necessary for the initial vision to be sustainable. Great leaders leave nothing to chance.

Dynamic Operating Systems

Great leaders translate their strategies into operating systems that dictate exactly how the company will do every aspect of what it does and exactly how the people in the company will do what they do. Detailed descriptions of the operating systems are documented in written operations manuals. The description of the systems are thorough, specific and relevant to deliver the experiences of the vision and create the foundation by which all goals will be achieved. This is the step that many leaders miss. Until operating systems based on strategies created are documented, you can not create clarity. Do not be a leader who neglects this crucial step. Operating systems are also considered dynamic to allow for continuous improvement.

Goals

Great leaders are relentless in using the company's strategically created systems to deliver their financial, customer satisfaction, and team-member satisfaction goals.

When implemented, this powerful five-step tool called the **LCP**, will bring clarity to your company and team and will guide you as you build a solid foundation for success. The process of the **LCP** as a whole looks like this: Filter and clarify your **Vision** through your core **Values** and define it in rigorous **Strategy** sessions.

Then translate your strategies into written, **Dynamic Operating Systems** that include accountability tools that measure performance towards your **Goals**.

When you use this process, stress will be lower because team members will know that they can stand on a strategic foundation as they reach for ever higher goals. Clarity will be high because team members know exactly what the company is trying to accomplish.

Another benefit of using the **LCP** is that when unexpected changes are required, they can be made without negatively impacting the current operations. Remarkably, this creates the opportunity for team members to synergize with other areas in the company, knowing that systemized operations are in place and producing predictable results with, or without, their constant oversight.

Leadership Chaos to Clarity will provide you with a systematic process to create clarity at all levels of your organization. Let us begin with the first step: **Vision**.

Leadership Tool Box

- The Leadership Clarity Pyramid
- Values are guideposts.
- Dynamic systems allow for continuous improvement.

PART 1
THE TOOLS

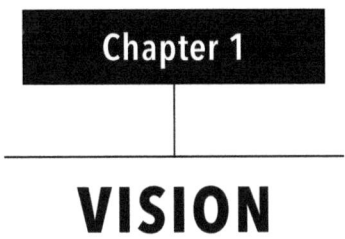

VISION

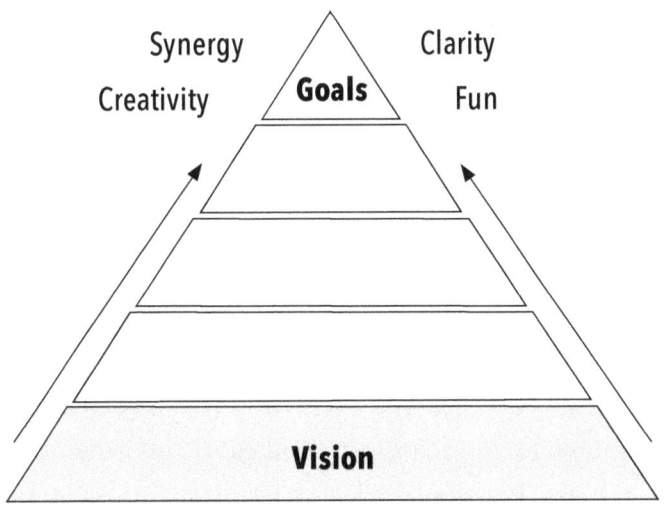

Leadership Clarity Pyramid©

What is your vision?

Every company begins with a vision. Someone somewhere has specific ideas about what experiences their company will provide for both customers and team members, and what financial results those experiential operations will deliver. If you can not answer this question, how do you and your team know if the company is delivering the correct outcomes? Team members want to follow great leaders, but great leaders must know where they are going and why they are going there.

At this level of the pyramid, the focus is on "what." The leader is visualizing what his or her department should *look* and *feel* like when it operates. They can *see* the customer experiences and *feel* the emotions of customers and team members. They have the beginnings of a keen understanding of crucial operational philosophies that will define where the company will focus. For example, leaders at this stage may describe their operations as fun, detailed, heartfelt, collaborative, engaging, colorful, experiential, laser-focused, thoughtful or many other terms that get at the heart of what will be delivered during operations.

For companies that have been around for a long time, you may have to go a long way back to discover who had the original vision – but, trust me, it's there. It may have been in drawings of a breakthrough or the design of a logo on a cocktail napkin, but someone was excited about a new way of doing things and began to define what it would look like.

The Oxford dictionary's definition of vision is: 1. "the faculty or state of being able to see" and 2. "the ability to plan or think about the future with imagination or wisdom." To be clear, this is not a **Vision Statement**. That will come later and can be a very useful tool to create clarity, especially if you include your people in the creation of the statement. This vision is a leader at any level of an organization *imagining* what experiences their portion of the business will provide as it operates at its best and is accomplishing all its goals.

To help you fully understand the difference between leadership "vision" and a "vision statement" let me share some examples of vision.

Imagine you and the love of your life have decided to get married and start a life together. You lovingly stare out the window and dream of the upcoming experiences of the wedding – the location, the guests, the dress and tux and so much more. You see the smiles and can feel the love in the room. You also think of a unique little house with a fenced-in backyard for your dog. You can see the property, the staircase to the second floor, the great kitchen with a gas stove, and the wonderful master-bathroom. You don't know how you will make it happen, and you are not worried about that now, but you can visualize the physical portion and feel the emotions that their achievement will invoke.

Here is another image of a vision. You have decided to go out to dinner at the fancy restaurant. You make the reservation and now begin to imagine how special you will feel when you arrive. You can visualize the entire sequential experience from the beginning to the end and how it smells, tastes, and makes you feel. The server will greet you right away. The drinks will be unique and tasty and come quickly. The decor will delight the senses. The room will be warm with great music. And so much more. At the end of the evening you will be sincerely thanked and asked to come back soon.

These short examples demonstrate the mental ability to see and feel experiences that will exist in the future, just as you can see and feel experiences that could happen in your company.

Now, let us look at an in-depth example that will illuminate an initial visioning process for leaders who are stepping in at the top. (In Chapter 7, Apply the Tools, we will review a simple exercise you can perform with your department heads since it is important that department leaders mirror the company-wide process. The exercise will help them create their own visions that are in alignment with the overall company vision. This is another way to clarify the company vision for team members at all levels.)

The Visioning Process in Action

You have just been hired as the general manager of a resort hotel. As you step into the role, you will be responsible for enacting and accomplishing a great many things. Here are a few key items that will assist you in using the vision portion of the **Leadership Clarity Pyramid**:

- Discuss the current vision and goals for the property with ownership
- Review current brand and positioning statements and agreements
- Review current and past financial goals and performance

- Look for current mission, vision, and value statements, if available
- Walk the property and speak with team members and guests
- "Secret shop" the property as a guest to experience all service areas.

Now, as the leader at the top of this organization, you must spend time reflecting on all that you have learned and experienced. Therefore, you must:

- Mentally compare your actual experiences with the brand level, public image, and current financial performance
- Take copious notes and score each experience
- Compare what you expected to occur with what actually happened
- List the experiences from best to worst.

While fresh in your mind, you may want to prioritize the areas that you currently believe will need to change first. Keep in mind that you are not trying to solve anything at this point; you are simply ruminating on the knowledge gained and experiences you encountered.

While your initial efforts will focus on completing the **LCP** for the entire resort, as a brief exercise on a separate piece of paper, list all the subordinate departments that will then complete their own. We will return to this exercise in Chapter 6, Create Clarity.

Remember, at this point, we are simply talking about the first level of the **LCP**: Vision. This is as entrepreneurial as it gets. Be incredibly creative as you visualize what operations will *look* like and *feel* like as they achieve success – it is about the experience of all involved. The actual nuts and bolts of how you will bring the vision to life will be determined in the *Strategy* section of the pyramid.

Here is a personal example of how the visioning process can work, or not work. Immediately upon being promoted from Athletic Director to General Manager of the venerable, and struggling, Indianapolis Athletic Club in 1999, and fresh off of training in the *Seven Habits of Highly Effective People* provided by Jim Johnson, the outstanding GM/COO of the Washington Athletic Club, I enthusiastically rolled out a new vision to my department heads. "Enthusiastically" may not be a strong enough word – think just worked out, double latte, Van Halen enthusiastic – maybe a little too fired up for the first introduction to the new approach.

The Club's operations were faltering as the membership rolls and revenue had been falling for years. Millions of dollars in deferred maintenance was catching up on us and the overall attitude of the team was neutral to poor, at best. My vision included a proactive, positive approach – thinking win/win – creating new, higher levels of accountability, and other exciting thoughts that I, as a young leader now leading 125 people, thought were great.

In my mind's eye, I could see a reinvigorated effort, focus and performance as we had achieved in the IAC Athletic Department since my arrival. The result? The executive assistant quit saying I was not the person for the job, and the clubhouse manager and executive chef turned in their notices. I was so excited to move the Club in a great direction. What went wrong?

Actually, two important things happened. One, I did not include my leadership team in the creation of the vision, and threw it at them with no time to prepare. That does not mean the vision was wrong. It means that I had not respected them enough to tap into their passion and expertise to help craft the vision that would guide the organization going forward. The second thing that happened was more positive. I invited everyone to come along on a journey to achieve the vision – but told them that if all the positive energy and new, higher levels of accountability were not for them, they would need to move on. And many did. Thank goodness.

While my approach was clumsy at best, it was authentic and heartfelt. In the long run it actually achieved what needed to be done. Leaders opted out who were never going to be in alignment with what needed to happen for the Club to radically improve its struggling performance. I did not want them to leave, but their leaving allowed me to create a team that could make the vision come to life instead of spending years wrestling with those who would never make it happen.

So, where does vision come from? Vision can come from a lot of places, or no place at all. In my experience, vision comes from education, personal life experiences, professional experiences and remaining open to knowledge and collaboration garnered from media, people and simply contemplation. One could make a case that it would be hard to have a vision for running a fine-dining restaurant, if you had never eaten in, worked in, or read about them. At the same time, a creative vision can strike like a lightning bolt. Perhaps the total lack of experience with fine-dining would lead to a way to achieve an operation that had never been thought of before.

Here is an example. If you study all the elements required to deliver a certain brand-level of a hotel, it does not take a rocket scientist to then go experience it and judge whether or not the hotel is delivering on the brand promise.

If you are just getting started as a leader or are switching industries, the vision may start with you; but figuring out how to deliver it will come from collaboration with those who have the knowledge you lack.

How do you know if the vision you have will work? The first thing to do is define "work." That could include, but not be limited to creating customer satisfaction, team-member satisfaction, improved products and services and, of course, profit. All those things will be determined as you fully complete the **Leadership Clarity Pyramid.**

Now that you have a grasp of the vision step in the **LCP** process, it is time to decide what values are most important to you, your customers, and your team as you deliver the experience of your vision. Let us now clarify your core values.

Leadership Tool Box

- LCP Vision
- The definition of Vision
- The Visioning Process
- "Secret Shopping" your operations
- Include your teams in the LCP process.
- "Invite" team members to join you in changing the status quo.
- Book Reference: *The Seven Habits of Highly Effective People* by Stephen Covey

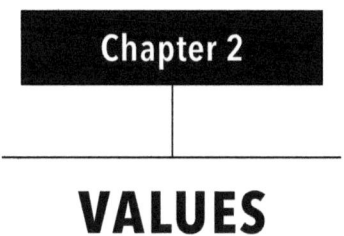

VALUES

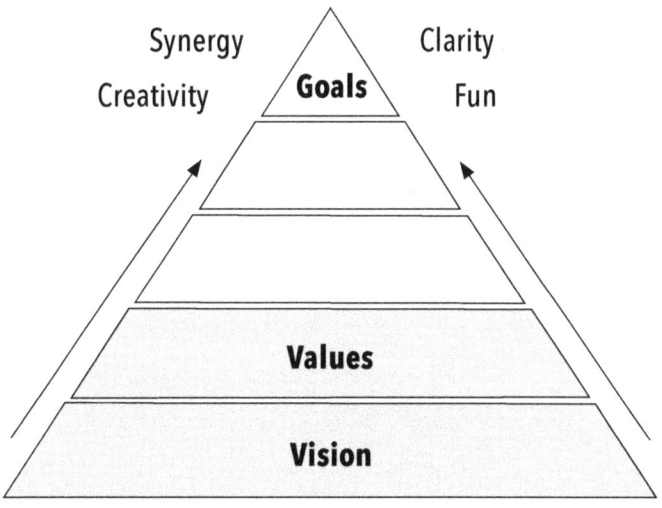

Leadership Clarity Pyramid©

Once you have outlined a vision of *what* is to be accomplished, it is time to decide what is most important about *how* it will be created and *how* it will run. You will be putting your "stakes in the ground," and these stakes will be your guideposts as you move up the **LCP** and eventually operate your company.

The biggest "stake" is the core set of values by which all aspects of your company will be governed. In an article from *Entrepreneur* magazine, marketing expert Kim T. Gordon wrote, "Today more than ever, customers want to know what your company stands for…." I agree with that, but it is not just customers who want to know – it is your team. The *key words* that make up your company's values may have the greatest impact on the quality of your business-life going forward.

Values create consistency and clarity of purpose, direction and accountability. Your customers and team members all crave consistency and predictability. Your new core values act as constant reminders of "the cause, the purpose and direction" of your company and can be easily cited when challenging, strategic decisions are required.

In other words, values inform all interested parties as to:

- What is important to you

- Who you are
- What you stand for
- Where you are going, and
- How you will make decisions

What are your company's values?

The goal at this point in the process is to select five or six words that will guide your future efforts. If you are starting a company by yourself, you can do this work by yourself. If you are doing this for an existing company or existing department within an existing company, you will want to include your team. More about how to do that is included in Chapter 3, Strategy, and Chapter 7, Apply the Tools, Leadership.

Prior to including your team, I suggest you start by thinking of categories of values that would be important to have defined prior to moving into strategy. These might include:

1. Behavioral
2. Qualitative
3. Quantitative
4. Aspirational
5. Philosophical

Now, brainstorm the values that might be most appropriate to your company in each category. Do not worry if they have been said or used before. Values are truths that will be recognized by all interested parties as statements of what you believe. However, I also suggest that you do not make them so bizarre that no one understands them.

Here are some possible examples:

1. Behavioral: Hard work, Positivity, Optimism, Commitment, Integrity, Honesty, Teamwork

2. Qualitative: Excellence, First-class, Best-in-class, Outstanding

3. Quantitative: Most, Number 1 Seller, Million Dollar, Profit, Margin Leader

4. Aspirational: Continuous improvement, Safest, Lowest Injuries, Industry Standard, Unique

5. Philosophical: Charitable, Community, Fun, Communication, Constructive Conflict, People First, Diverse

Once you have some values created by category, it is time to reduce them to a manageable amount. Do not discard any of them. Try to get them down to one or two from each category – and maybe one bonus value that resonates so strongly with you that you would not think of moving forward without it. For now, this is taking your vision and placing key touchstones to guide you as you begin to bring your vision to life in the next steps of the **LCP**.

Whenever possible, include your team. Within a month of becoming the General Manager at Trophy Club Country Club, I had all-team meetings on the schedule. I wanted to introduce myself, have some fun, show them the **LCP**, review current performance, and invite everyone to join me on a journey to take the Club's operations and performance from where it currently was to a much higher level. "We're going from here to here." I gestured my arm from waist level to over my head. "We're going for the thin air. And I want you all to come along." I then asked, "Why do you think we have to go there?"

Some good answers came from the team. "To make more money." "To provide a better experience for our members." It is always great to have team members actively participate in team meetings. Sometimes they will volunteer responses, other times you will need to select specific people and ask for a reply.

I then answered my own question. "We have to go there because the competition is tough. Life is short and we all want to make more money and share more success, and enjoy our work lives. In addition, the home office demands it. So, now I want to invite each of you to be a part of something amazing. Something very special. We can't do it without you, and your leadership team will do whatever is necessary to provide you with an environment to be incredibly successful. That includes more consistent accountability for everyone, especially the leaders."

My style is to state the obvious – over and over. I am sure this drives some team members a bit crazy; but I never want a team member to say that they did not know or were not told the full story. This technique borrows from Sandler Sales Training's "Upfront Contract" concept. Give them full clarity and understanding upfront. If they do not want to participate, okay. It is best to know that early on.

Next in the meeting, I ask for the team's help. "Please help us select the values that will guide our efforts as we achieve great things. On the table are paper and pens. Please anonymously share three values that you think should be a part of this journey."

The results were amazing. While I already had several that I knew were non-negotiable, the team's contributions far exceeded my expectations. After the meeting, I tallied the suggestions on a spreadsheet noting how many times each individual value had been suggested. Then working with the leadership team, we used three that were most often suggested in our final six values: Communication, Integrity and Teamwork. The leadership team added these three values: Continuous Improvement, Excellence and Fun.

Does it get any better than that? A diverse group of team members contributed their honest opinions that would help the company, and them, succeed. Thinking back on the process elicits strong emotions of appreciation and affection. We then posted the spreadsheet of the suggestions by the time clock for all to see. When teams are given the chance to contribute and are appreciated for their efforts, they respond very positively.

Once completed, we created business cards with our vision and new values and distributed them to every team member. What a great team I had inherited. As my Food and Beverage Director, Amy Masey says, "People don't come to work to fail." This was certainly true with this group. That does not mean everyone will remain a part of the team as the expectations are raised; but it does mean that a process has begun that authentically recognizes and appreciates the value of each person.

In summary, your company's core values will permeate every aspect of how your company operates and will create consistency in the actions and reactions you take as its leader. Now, armed with a solid vision and the values that will guide you, it is time to figure out how you will bring the operation together in the Strategy portion of the **LCP**.

Leadership Tool Box

- LCP Values
- Values create clarity.
- The leader makes the final decisions.
- Authentic appreciation is powerful.
- Upfront Contract *Sandler Sales Training*
- Discussion point from Amy Masey: "People don't come to work to fail."

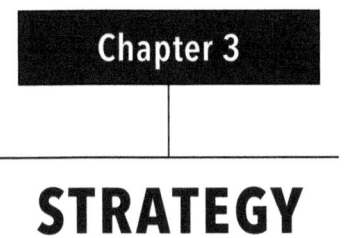

STRATEGY

Leadership Clarity Pyramid©

Okay. Now things get difficult – or fun – depending on your idea of fun. In step three, you and your team will get both creative and specific as you figure out how to deliver every aspect of your vision, while also delivering the financial results necessary to sustain the company. In other words, your focus must be on determining if you can deliver the original operational vision, which is now guided by your core values, while also achieving the financial goals required.

My family is very entrepreneurial. The last three generations of Rowes have run their own businesses and we have developed a saying, "It's not whether or not a business is mismanaged, but how mismanaged." Why is this true? Because you are dealing with ever-changing people, technology, society, pressure, financial performance, the economy and so many other factors. Once you understand this concept, that some level of mismanagement almost always exists, you can start honestly digging into your operations without blaming anyone for its current condition. And that is what this step in the **Leadership Clarity Pyramid** is all about.

So, ask yourself. How can you use strategic thinking to define your systems and reduce mis-management?

Creating new strategies that will materially improve operations and results may take a great deal of time and effort, depending on the complexity of your current operations, talent of your team, and goals. In this chapter we will discuss several important, but more general, points necessary to accomplish this step. Then in Chapter 9 we will take a close look at what needs to be done to implement strategy sessions for departments looking to make specific improvements.

Before moving on and looking at an example of what strategy development looks like, allow me to point out that, depending on the size of your company or department and its current status, it is very likely that one strategy session will not generate every bit of structure, creativity, and clarity needed to achieve the new levels of performance required. Take the pressure off and prioritize your focus. Choose your highest-priority areas and complete them before moving on. This will allow you to create momentum and demonstrate the effectiveness of the effort.

Once you address your initially identified, high-priority areas, and you have implemented dynamic operating systems that are showing measurable improvements, you will have a model for action that can be replicated as often as is needed.

There may also be several levels of strategy sessions that need to occur, depending on the state of your company or department. Starting from easiest to most difficult, they may include, but are not limited to:

1. **Simply blowing the dust off your current systems to ensure their continued relevance and validity.** Clarity is created when you take a close look at how well your current written systems document how you and your people do what you do. Announce to the entire company that these prioritized strategy meetings will happen, and that you will share any updates immediately with everyone.

2. **Executing a gap-analysis on old systems and filling the gaps with new systems that clearly communicate how you and your people do what you do.** In this slightly more difficult example, you have found that system descriptions about how you do things do not exist, or are completely irrelevant to how you are actually accomplishing the tasks. As previously mentioned, take care to select the highest priority area or department and then accurately complete all the systems required to fill the gaps.

3. **Working on systems that are producing a sub-par product.** In this situation you will need to look at the processes you and your people use to imagine, create and distribute your product. There will be a demand for critical thinking and transparency as the team takes a deep dive into areas and processes that are proving ineffective. The written systems are present but the end result of their use is a product that is not performing.

4. **Perhaps most difficult are strategy sessions focused on evaluating situations where the required financial results are not met**. Honest and sometimes brutal discussions may be necessary to determine where the problem resides:

   - Is there pricing pressure from new competition?
   - Has your product quality fallen? If so, why?
   - Have you lost market share? If so, why?
   - Are costs exceeding budget?
   - Is your payroll exceeding budgeted payroll?
   - Is your sales and marketing team producing the performance required?

These, and perhaps many more areas, will need to be intensely evaluated to identify what has occurred and what to do about it.

To illustrate the strategy process, let us go back to our example of you becoming the general manager of a resort hotel. Since the vision focuses on the end product, which is the operation of a resort hotel and its achieving appropriate financial results, we will tackle that first. Your job in the strategy portion of the **Leadership Clarity Pyramid** is to analyze operational areas, and define for all interested parties how your systems and people will deliver the vision down to the minutia. Eat this "elephant" one bite at a time and start your strategy sessions with the areas you deemed to be the highest priority.

For this example, let us assume that you have determined that the food and beverage operations are a high priority for overall guest satisfaction and financial performance, and they are not achieving their customer satisfaction and financial goals. In the strategy session be sure the appropriate team members are available, as well as current systems descriptions, financial reports, satisfaction survey scores, comparable market surveys, brand standards and any other data or tools you feel will be helpful. Let the team members who will participate know in advance what will happen and how they can prepare. Here is an example of some of the questions you will need to answer:

1. **Branding and positioning**
   - Is the resort's food and beverage operation delivering experiences that are consistent with the brand requirements?
2. **Financial performance** – the financials tell a story. What story are your resort's food and beverage financial results telling?
   - Review with the group:
     - Cover counts per meal period, per outlet
     - Average sale per cover, per meal period, per outlet
     - Percent of sales from food, liquor, beer, wine, non-alcoholic drinks
     - Satisfaction survey scores
     - The current organizational chart – what should it be? Job descriptions, task lists, continuous training, compensation.
     - Labor percentage of gross sales
     - Food Cost, Liquor Cost, Beer Cost, Wine Cost
     - Recent Capital Improvements
     - Current Menus and Pricing

- Secret Shopping Reports
- Current branding per outlet and marketing efforts both on and off property
- Vendor relationships – are you getting the best products at the best prices?

This should give you a good idea of what the strategy step looks like. However, two extremely important questions must be asked in order to focus the energy of the group:

1. Are the current, written operating systems truly reflected in the operations of the department?
2. Do the current systems consistently and accurately deliver the vision and financial goals?

In my 40 years of experience, I have discovered that the written operating systems for most companies have become irrelevant. They are either on a computer and never viewed, or in binders somewhere collecting dust. The actual operation is running in some vague, inconsistent, and hybrid manner that is over-reliant on the memory of team members.

If you answered *Yes* to question #1 above, move to question #2. If your answer here is also *Yes*, then ask: is your vision still valid and delivering the financial and other results that are desired. If *No*, it is time to move to the next step in the **Leadership Clarity Pyramid***:* Dynamic Operating Systems.

If you answered *No* to question #1, FIRST, answer question #2. If you are lucky, somehow the operations have morphed into a better delivery of the vision, even if those changes were never memorialized in the official written operating systems. In this case, as a part of both the strategy and dynamic operating systems steps, compare your written systems to the actual performance of the department, and start rewriting the systems based on the successful, actual operation.

Review everything and use data. Clarity relies upon your relentless commitment to this effort. This will be an interesting and valuable time of discovery for all involved. If, however, you are in a position where your written systems are not represented in the daily operations *and* fail to deliver the vision, you will need to take your current written operating systems and strategize where they fall short. First, in an all-inclusive strategy session, evaluate and document where the current written systems fall short of delivering the vision, then rewrite the systems in their entirety based on the best-possible strategies – not consensus.

As previously mentioned, while your team may offer several great ideas, it may not be possible to use them all. Since you, as the leader, will ultimately be held responsible for the performance of the company, you must make the final choice. Great leaders will make that choice and assure the team that should the choice that is made not deliver the required results, the other great ideas will be revisited.

Now that new strategic initiatives have been discovered and analyzed to ensure their efficacy for creating the required operational improvement, it is time to memorialize those strategies in your written operating systems. Chapter 4 will discuss why formally adding your new strategies to current operating systems is so important and how to roll those new systems out to be sure team members are implementing them as intended.

Leadership Tool Box

- The LCP Strategy
- Strategy work is entrepreneurial.
- All businesses are mismanaged to some degree.
- Ask, "Where are the written operating systems?"

DYNAMIC OPERATING SYSTEMS

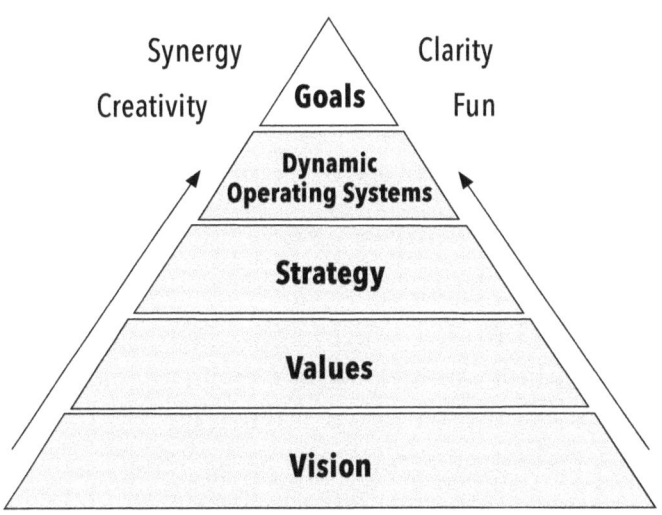

Leadership Clarity Pyramid©

In order to move from chaos to clarity, great leaders document their operational strategies in written and dynamic operating systems manuals. This is the step many leaders miss. They may have excellent ideas and strategies, but for some inexplicable reason, they neglect to write them down. Whenever I have applied for a new leadership role, I ask the current administration, "Can you please show me your written operating systems?" Amazingly, the answer that I have most often received is, "I've got them all right here," as the responder points to their head indicating that they have memorized everything they need to know and do not have a written version.

When I receive that answer from any or all the departments within the potential new assignment, I know I am going to be incredibly successful. Why? Well, it is simple – because one of the first tasks I will require is that each department head create written operating manuals that describe their current systems of operation. As you will read later in this chapter, that exercise alone will produce clarity and improvement. Beginning with this task also creates a basis for continued improvement should the newly-produced, written systems demonstrate significant weaknesses in that department's operational effectiveness.

What do your written operating systems say?

Do your written operations manuals match your actual operations?

The value of creating or improving your company's operations manuals is multifold. On the one hand, the manuals create a communication tool that becomes the common language of the standards by which all performance will be measured. Additionally, the detailed process of their creation is usually a time of incredible discovery. You may hear leaders say things like, "Wow, I didn't know we were doing it like that." or "This is crazy; our systems aren't even close to how we actually do things."

Your company's written operating systems are a means for you to define and communicate how you do every facet of what you do. They are imperative in order to create clarity for your team members. They lower stress because team members know the systems they use are both relevant to the company's vision and strategies, and in alignment with the company's values.

The team members also understand how their efforts, combined with these systems of operation, will help them and the company be successful. This clarity contributes to team-member satisfaction – and satisfied team members are highly productive and stay put.

As each department completes these high-priority strategy sessions, and translates the new strategies and ideas into fresh, relevant, dynamic operating systems, be sure to refer to your pre-set timelines in your project management software. This ensures that the drafts of the new systems are created on schedule. These first drafts will not be perfect, and they do not have to be perfect. However, they must clearly represent everything that is done in the department and include the new ideas that were agreed upon.

A company's systems are dynamic because the need for change and continuous improvement is inevitable. Here is where so many companies fail. First, the systems currently written are not fully and accurately expressed in the day-to-day operations of the business. Second, when it is determined that a change must be made in how a portion of the business is run, and if the actual written systems are not accurate, it is difficult to know where to target your change. If your operations map is inaccurate, how do you know where you went wrong?

Also, since the systems are not functional, team members may, or may not, be trained in the new operational directives. If they are, and it is only done verbally, accuracy will be lost. The accountability measures are vague and people-reliant, rather than systematic.

Without the clarity and accountability of written systems, it is quite likely that the performance of the team will return to the pre-update behavior. Any improvements that might have been gained are lost – and it is not the team member's fault. If this lack of compliance with systems continues for any extended period of time, you can expect that the company is adrift. At that point, you have become over-reliant on the memory of team members – and, heaven forbid if they ever decide to leave.

Now you know there is a better way – a way to move from chaos to clarity – the **Leadership Clarity Pyramid**. When your company or department discovers a new or better way to operate whether through well-planned and run strategy sessions, or simply due to a team member's suggestion, the first thing to do is update the written, Dynamic Operating Systems Manuals.

Then, the next steps are:

- Save the written and updated system component with revision dates in the footer
- Distribute to all team members who are governed by the change
- Schedule group training to review the change
- Schedule first-person training for everyone and continue training until all have mastered the new approach
- Regularly inspect team member performance to ensure they are properly performing the task in alignment with the updated system
- Measure the success of the change.

Once completed, you now have both an updated system and an updated operational delivery that match. Continuous improvement has occurred. Do this time and time again and, as you reflect on your company over time, you will see that the operations have matured, and continuous improvement to your dynamic systems is delivering higher levels of performance than those initially achieved.

Sometimes moving from *Leadership Chaos to Clarity* relies on the simplest of efforts done equally well by ALL departments. The following is one of those simple efforts that is so often neglected – formatting the operating systems manuals and computer folders.

The days of binders and printed manuals are gone for most companies. While I always liked seeing the binders proudly displayed for all to see in leaders' offices, I am happy to be saving trees. Now, we use our computers and print only as needed. Thanks to Microsoft and other word processing software, the storage systems they created mirror the old tabbed binders. With this in mind, your electronically-stored, written operating systems should be organized as though in a tabbed binder. Here is an example of the e-formatting of a Dynamic Operating Systems. Note that every document should be in a subfolder.

Level One Folder Name: My Company

1. **Finance**
   - 📁 Budgets and Budgeting
     - 📁 2022 Budget
     - 📁 2021 Budget and Actuals
   - 📁 Forecasting
   - 📁 Cash Flow Monitoring

2. **Accounting**
   - 📁 Accounts Payable
   - 📁 Accounts Receivable
   - 📁 Payroll
   - 📁 Banking

3. **Marketing**
   - 📁 Budget and Goals
   - 📁 Online Strategies and Results
   - 📁 Networking Strategies and Results

4. **Sales**
   - 📁 Budget and Goals
   - 📁 Comparative Market Analysis
   - 📁 Sales Performance Measurement Systems

5. **Human Resources**
   - 📁 Payroll and Benefits
     - 📁 Organizational Chart
     - 📁 Job Descriptions
     - 📁 Task Lists
   - 📁 Annual Reviews

6. **Legal**
    - 📁 Licenses and Contracts
    - 📁 Current Issues

7. **Facilities and Maintenance**
    - 📁 Preventative Maintenance
    - 📁 Daily Task Lists
    - 📁 Capital Projects
    - 📁 Budget

8. **Product Specifications**
    - 📁 Proprietary Product Data
    - 📁 Manufacturing Specs
    - 📁 Vendors

9. **Customer Feedback**
    - 📁 Annual Surveys
    - 📁 Emails and Letters
    - 📁 Data

10. **Strategic Planning**
    - 📁 Short Term Plans
    - 📁 Budgets
    - 📁 Long Term Plans

This example gives you a clear concept of how your virtual binder is put together. There could be many, many subfolders needed to properly "file" all your documents within a certain topic and that is fine – whatever works best for you and your company. What you do not want is hundreds of unfiled documents accumulating in any level of subfolder. When that happens you spend valuable time searching for documents instead of accomplishing tasks.

When done correctly by your entire team, this simple task can quickly begin moving you from chaos to clarity. If you are totally committed to creating an environment for your people to be incredibly successful, audit your leadership's computer storage of records and documents. It is not a matter of trust. It is you, requiring the best from your team leaders.

Each step in the **Leadership Clarity Pyramid** has built upon the previous step. With rock solid step four completed, we now move from dynamic operating systems to goals. The achievement of the company's goals will be the reward for your investment.

Leadership Tool Box

- LCP Dynamic Operating Systems
- Team members + Systems = Outcomes
- Written systems create accountability.
- Example of a real-life Systems organization

GOALS

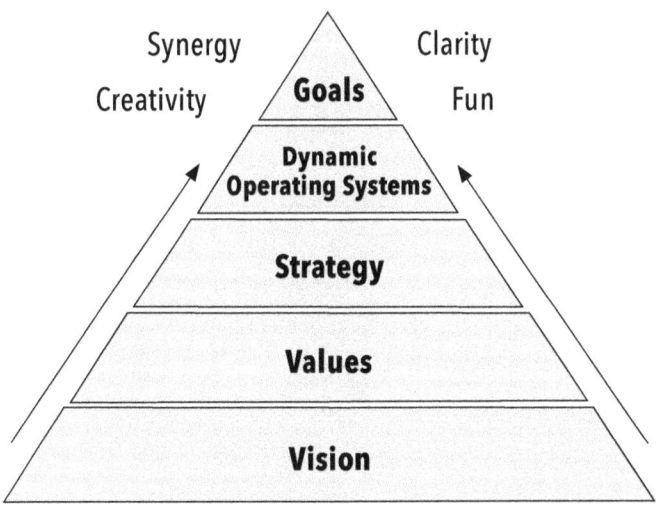

Leadership Clarity Pyramid©

What are your goals and how do you measure them?

Simply put, the goals of a business are to deliver specific and measurable results in a consistent and predictable fashion that allows for the vision to be realized. When this is happening, your team will be energized. They will be positioned to have fun, think creatively about continuous improvements, and look to synergize with other departments because their department is performing well.

You might hear your team describe the operation as a "well-oiled machine." You, as the leader, can now focus on appreciating your team members and engaging them in new strategic discussions. You are now spending your time investing in and empowering your team to enjoy their roles and grow as professionals.

Once again, your company's or department's goal is to sustainably deliver its vision by delivering the necessary financial, customer-satisfaction, and team member satisfaction results.

The Goals step sits on top of the other four steps because the first four steps of vision, values, strategy and dynamic operating systems create a rock solid foundation on which your company can achieve its goals. When the first four steps are in alignment and delivering predictable results, your team can confidently stand upon that foundation, and continually reach for higher goals. The day-to-day operations are functional, predictable, consistent and effective. Clarity is present – leaders are leading – and team members are performing according to the operating systems manuals, while also keen to improve the department if opportunities present themselves.

As a leader, your challenge is to regularly compare your current operational results with your goals. Are you achieving them? If you are not achieving your goals, is your level of achievement enough to sustain the company or department? If not, you will need to go back to the strategy level of the **LCP** to develop new ways to operate that give you the greatest chance of achieving the necessary results to continue.

Let us take a look at a few examples of Key Performance Indicators (KPI) that could serve as your company's goals. It is crucial to create both the goals and the measurement tools to ensure that you have accurate data that shows you how your company or department is performing towards achieving those goals.

Financial KPI

- Gross Revenue – a good starting point – easy for everyone to understand and a good number to watch for overall growth
- EBITDA – earnings before interest, taxes, depreciation and amortization
  - Earnings: Net income or loss of a company
  - Interest: The cost of borrowing money
  - Taxes: Payments to the government
  - Depreciation: Reduction of the value of physical assets over their useful life
  - Amortization of intangibles which may include goodwill, debt issuance costs, etc.
- Cost of Goods Sold (COGS) – the cost you pay for the products you sell
- Payroll as a Percent of Gross Revenue – a good way to monitor overall payroll
- Operating Expenses as a Percent of Gross Revenue – another high-level way to monitor performance
- Revenue Growth
- New Customer Acquisition Cost – the sales and marketing cost of a new customer

Customer Satisfaction KPI

- Customer Satisfaction Survey Scores – you need customer feedback without turning customers off
- Percent of Repeat Customers – may be a good indicator of satisfied customers

Team Member Satisfaction KPI

- Team Member Satisfaction Scores
- Annual Percent of Team Member Turnover

Sales and Marketing KPI

- Total Marketing Expense as a Percent of Gross Revenue
- Open Rates, CTR, CPC – focused on online marketing
- Total Leads – from all sources
- Cost Per Lead
- Lead to Close Ratio – monitoring the performance of sales people is crucial

When I was the general manager at Pelican Isle Yacht Club, we had an outstanding finance committee chairperson who had been an accountant with KPMG for 32 years. His favorite line was, "The numbers tell a story." I have found that mindset to be extremely helpful in interpreting financial performance. So, as you choose your company's KPI, and format your financial reports, be sure that they tell a true, clarity-producing story. You are not looking to manipulate the numbers. You just need to quickly and easily understand the story they tell, and know where to look if you need to dig into a specific area for further explanation.

The measurement tools should be timely (daily, weekly, monthly, quarterly, annually), but perhaps most importantly, whenever possible, available in real time. The better your teams monitor their performance against previously established goals, the better likelihood they will achieve them – or, if not achieve them, sound the alarm bell as soon as the forecasted performance appears to fall short.

Your leadership tool box now carries the **LCP** tools. Before moving on to how you use those tools, let us review the five steps of the **Leadership Clarity Pyramid**.

1. You have a solid understanding of how *vision* will guide all future efforts to achieve your desired outcomes.

2. You know how *values* will help to inform all interested parties of what is important to your company.
3. You see how you must conduct rigorous *strategy* sessions to discover the approaches that will deliver the company you desire.
4. You know you must translate all your strategies into *written operating systems* to cement the strategic efforts.
5. And finally, you know that the *goals* sit upon this foundation of clarity and strength, and must deliver both the envisioned operation and the measurable results.

I hope you are as excited as I am by the results that this clarity-generating tool can provide you and your company: fewer hours for you, smarter use of your teams, achievement of KPI, and achievement of work and life balance. These benefits and more are available to you.

Before moving on to the application of the **LCP**, please remember that this strategy represents you proactively changing the status-quo. After implementation, your company will see a clear pathway to operations with greatly reduced chaos. It will not happen without effort or heart. Why not go for the thin air – the place where only eagles dare? You and your future are worth it. Take a breath – settle in – and let us look at how to apply everything you have just learned and take your company from chaos to clarity.

Leadership Tool Box

- LCP Goals
- KPI Examples
- "The numbers tell a story."
- Accurate data creates clarity.
- Your LCP goals sit on a foundation of vision, values and strategy.

PART 2
APPLICATION

Chapter 6

CREATE CLARITY

In the most successful companies and organizations *all* team members have the same level of understanding about what the company is trying to accomplish. Unfortunately, most companies are unsuccessful in cascading their critical messaging from the top of the organization to the bottom – including verbal, written and non-verbal messaging. Do not minimize the value of non-verbal communication. Studies have proven that body language can be far more influential than verbal communication. Clarity may be high among the executive leadership who meet regularly and have direct access to the vision creators; but the lower-level leadership and front-line team members are not getting the message. In addition, in the absence of a clear story, team members will create their own – and, more often than not, their stories will be very different than that of leadership.

Why is cascading of critical messaging not accomplished? In my most recent experience as general manager at Trophy Club Country Club, I found that mid-level leaders often fail to share with their subordinate leaders and team members what is shared with them. It may be that they are too busy, they do not have the skills to translate the message effectively, or they are simply not fully onboard. Strategies we used to improve sharing important messages at TCCC included:

1. Providing written notes for key messages that could be posted or copied and shared,
2. Using the "GroupMe" text messaging software for communicating directly to specific teams within the Club,
3. Including less than senior-level leadership in meetings to provide the messaging to multiple levels at one time, and
4. Completing a final, five minute meeting review to sum-up all key messages that were expected to be shared.

Many times in our weekly senior leadership team meetings I would say, "If what we've talked about here in this meeting doesn't leave this room, we're failing as leaders." So, to truly achieve company clarity you *must* include everyone. Let us take a look at who that may include.

Returning to the resort hotel example in Chapter 1, let us review the resort's departments that would benefit from the use of the **Leadership Clarity Pyramid**.

Here are a few of those departments:

- Food and Beverage
- Housekeeping and Laundry
- Maintenance
- Groundskeeping
- Marketing
- Sales
- Revenue Management
- Reservations
- Recreation
- Front desk
- Accounting
- Gift shop
- Security
- People Operations

All departments can benefit from the use of the **LCP** process. Repeating the **LCP** process in each department may seem redundant or overkill; but from my experience, you will not achieve the very best performance for your company without it.

It comes back to the fact that most companies are weak at cascading important messaging down the vertical silos. Instead, they conduct executive-level, strategic retreats and leave the sessions energized and full of clarity; then they return to their normal routine and neglect to invest the necessary time and energy to share the same level of clarity and energy with their teams. Do not let that happen to you. Make sure your strategic efforts do not stop until you have included all levels of the team in order to maximize their potential results.

For the greatest success with the **LCP** Tools, include the input of team members who will be governed by the results. This allows you to gain from their experience and achieve their buy-in. A strong leader will use their expertise to include everyone and ensure accomplishments are in alignment with the overarching vision of the company itself. In essence, each subsequent vision will expand on the overall company vision, but remain relevant to the specific function of the department.

To further illustrate the importance of including all team members in discussions of critical strategies and messaging, I refer to Jim Collins' fantastic book, *Good to Great*. He shares how the companies that succeeded in achieving great results demonstrated a commitment to **First Who, Then What**. The great companies hired the right people into the company, and then made sure they were intimately involved with deciding the direction of the company. In other words, they got the right people on the bus, the wrong people off the bus, and the right people in the right seats.

Once that was accomplished, the right people, in the right seats, contributed to the direction of their company or their department. *Good to Great* describes this important sequence as a portion of three sequential disciplined efforts – first, **disciplined people,** then **disciplined thought** and finally, **disciplined action.** Whenever possible, this should be your goal as well.

Leadership Tool Box

- Tools to improve message sharing
- Cascaded messaging is influenced by body language.
- In the absence of a story, team members will create their own concept.
- Study First Who, Then What in *Good to Great* by Jim Collins

Chapter 7

APPLY THE TOOLS, PHASE 1 LEADERSHIP

There are many ways to implement the **Leadership Clarity Pyramid** tools. In this and the next two chapters, is an example of one way that has, over time, proven to be extremely effective. Here in Chapter 7, Phase 1, we focus on actions the leaders will take to prepare themselves for a company-wide LCP process rollout. Then, in Chapter 8, Phase 2, we will shift the focus to rallying the team at an All-Team LCP Rollout Meeting. Finally, in Chapter 9, we will take a close look at the subsequent LCP processes for individual departments. These processes will ultimately deliver strategically updated, written operating systems that will reduce chaos, increase clarity, and deliver your KPI. Here is a general overview of the sequence:

Chapter 7, Phase 1

   I.   Prepare. As the leader of this process, you must be ready.
   II. Prepare the executive leadership, individually, to be onboard and ready.
   III. Create a base for success with executive leadership as a group.

Chapter 8, Phase 2

   I.   Rally the team at an all-team meeting. Collect suggestions for values, vision and improvement strategies.
   II. Post all-team meeting results.

Chapter 9, Strategy to Systems

Use the work completed in the strategic sessions to write and improve systems of operation – implement and measure outcomes.

While this is a very specific sequence, do what works best for you based on the position you occupy and the needs of your company. You may choose to sequence the process differently or use individual tools rather than all of them. Perhaps you already have excellent vision and value statements that are clearly understood by everyone in your company. Or, you may already know the departments that need strategic improvement and feel that moving straight to those efforts is the best course of action.

I caution you that moving from *Leadership Chaos to Clarity* requires that all team members are involved. If strategic changes are to be made in a specific silo, be sure all team members in that silo have clarity about what is happening, why it is happening, and the expected outcomes of the effort. It is important that everyone knows that you are leading your teams to a new level of performance, and all will be involved and benefit from the improvement.

Great things are about to happen for you and your team with you as the catalyst – better communication, more appreciation, better results, less stress. You are moving your company from *chaos to clarity*. Congratulations, in advance.

As a reminder, if you are at the top of the organization, the first result should be the **LCP** process fully completed for the company. The company-wide work should then be used as a guide by each department as they use the LCP. This ensures that subsequent efforts are in alignment with the company vision, values and strategies.

While this process is not rocket science, it is not easy. Be an excellent communicator – be authentic, self-effacing, disciplined, inclusive, committed, and include relentless follow-through until each team has completed its work. Actions will speak much louder than words – be ready to set the standard. Whatever the standard is, your people will look to you to demonstrate a 100% commitment to it.

Here is an overview of the Phase 1 processes for using the LCP tool:

I. **Prepare. As the ultimate leader of this process, you must be ready.**

    A. Review the LCP process

B. Create a first-draft timeline
   C. Set goals for the effort
   D. Write a first draft of vision and values

II. **Prepare your executive leadership, individually, to be onboard and ready.**
   A. Introduce them to the LCP process
   B. Discuss why the LCP process is necessary
   C. Make a commitment to your team
   D. Answer questions
   E. Ask for their enthusiastic commitment to the LCP effort

III. **Create a base for success with executive leadership as a group.**
   A. Probe for, and work through, any dissent
   B. Complete the Leadership Team Exercise #1 – Vision
   C. Vision vs. Actual Tool
   D. Complete the Leadership Team Exercise #2 – Values
   E. Complete the Leadership Team Exercise #3 - LCP Process and Timeline Review
   F. Conduct a Q&A until everything is out on the table

Let us now take a look at each of the Phase 1 steps.

I. Prepare. As the ultimate leader of this process, you must be ready.

A. Review the LCP process

Before you begin to include your team, it is important to fully familiarize yourself with the LCP process. To aid this process, start by writing a sequential outline that includes all the steps you plan to achieve. Visualize how you will accomplish each task and what it will feel like when it is completed. Get into personal alignment with those efforts. This will help you project authenticity when you orchestrate the process.

B. Create a first-draft timeline

Start a project management chart so that you can see how the LCP process will flow over time and how the different efforts will flow in relationship to each other. Account for holidays, key dates for departments and other potential delays. Do not set yourself up to fail by creating a timeline that has no chance of working – even if it is a first draft that you will revise many times before initiation of the LCP process company-wide.

C. Set goals for the effort

What, in your words, are the goals of this process implementation? What goals will you achieve along the way? How will the entire company be different when completed? What KPI will change and by how much? If you are going to invest your company's valuable time and energy into this effort, you want to know where it will take you. Actually seeing the goals that could be achieved should get you excited by the potential.

D. Write a first draft of vision and values

Prepare yourself – write your vision. Try to get everything out of your mind and on to paper. For your vision, it is not important that you focus on grammar – just get the specifics down.

To assist you, answer the following questions:

- What emotions does your operation evoke from customers?
- What feelings does your visioned operation evoke from team members?

- What characteristics will be present as your visioned company or department operates?
- What are key outcomes of your vision?
- What is the purpose of your visioned operation?
- What are your financial and other goals for the visioned operation?

Write six words that you currently believe should be the company's values. Of those, which ones are non-negotiable? For me, I insist on having "Continuous Improvement" as a company value because it sets the stage for continuous evaluation of strategies and systems compared to actual performance.

Now, as you move into the process of leading your team to deliver your vision, keep this outline in your mind – but do not share it all yet. First, let others be just as creative as you, and subtly guide them in the process.

If your current role is as a department head, and the company will not be using the **LCP**, use the current company mission, vision and value statements or credo to guide your efforts as you complete the pyramid. This will ensure the completed work is in full alignment with the company's vision and goals.

II. Prepare your executive leadership individually.

A. Introduce them to the LCP process

Meet with your leadership team members individually to introduce the idea of radically improving clarity at your company by using the LCP. Show them the **Leadership Clarity Pyramid** and let them know how important they are to the success of the effort and company. Explain your vision for using this tool to improve the company.

B. Discuss why the LCP process is necessary

Discuss what will be necessary, including where the company is now and where it must go. Assure them that this has nothing to do with blaming anyone for how the company currently operates.

C. Make a commitment to your team

Commit to creating an environment for them personally, and their department, to be incredibly successful. Let them know that you have some thoughts on goals that might be achieved but will leave that for discussion at the all-leadership team meeting that will be coming soon.

D. Answer questions

Ask if they have any questions. Thoroughly discuss all the implications of executing this important effort.

E. Ask for their enthusiastic commitment to the LCP effort

While this may sound corny, there are two cliches that really speak to what needs to be happening at this point. If you are comfortable with it, use these two cliches:

- "We need everyone pulling in the same direction if we have any chance of radically improving."
- "This effort will be challenging. We truly need to have all our arrows pointing in the same direction."

Why use these? It's very simple – because they are true. If you are going to lead your company to achieve <u>remarkable</u> results while also delivering quality of life for the team members, you will need everyone fully engaged in the effort. This does not mean that every idea from every leader will be used – only that you will ensure that *every idea* will be *heard* and *respected*. It is that respect that will ensure buy-in, and allow good leaders to align themselves with your efforts.

Next, look them in the eye and sincerely *invite* them to participate in the journey to higher-quality outcomes. If they are not up for the effort, now is the time to know. I have never had anyone opt out at this point, but do not be surprised if you lose some of your leadership team. Be prepared for it. It is not their fault or necessarily a bad thing. It may, however, slow down your progress until a full team of leaders is in place.

III. Create a base for success with executive leadership as a group.

A. Probe for, and work through, any dissent

Meet with all your remaining direct-report leadership together and let them know that you will expect 100% participation and commitment to the amazing journey that is coming. At this point, you are seeking to have your team be both open and honest, and to vigorously participate in the journey and bring the very best they have to offer. Ask each leader in the group to voice their concerns – yes, go one-by-one around the room. Encourage them to voice all the doubts and worries now, otherwise they will surface later, inhibit progress, and potentially cause damage. I like to say, "There's no way that my idea is perfect as it now sits. Tell me what I've missed. Beat it up." Every leader in attendance must make comments regarding your plan. It does no good if all that talent in the room says nothing.

B. Complete the Leadership Team Exercise #1 - Vision

At a specially scheduled meeting with your department heads, assign them the task to describe their vision for their department when it is operating at its best. I suggest this assignment be completed as follows:

1. Each leader has a maximum of five minutes.
2. Their description must be out loud.
3. They must describe what they see when they walk into their departments.
4. Their descriptions must include a great deal of descriptive language that communicates the look, feel, performance, focus and anything else that helps them paint a clear picture of a department that is producing outstanding results.

5. Take notes – be sure to jot down the keywords that are most important. After each leader has completed their time, make comments and ask for others to comment.
6. Finally, ask each leader to write copious notes on what they said and submit to you within 24 hours of the meeting.

C. Vision vs. Actual Tool

Here is an **important tool** for you to use when making changes. The actual experiences that are occurring in an existing operation will usually be different than what you or your team visualized. Maybe the experiences were better or maybe worse. As a leader, you must use this knowledge as a means to analyze operating systems to determine why. Some questions that you should ask include:

1. Were the differences within a tolerable variance?
2. If they were better, should systems be updated to reflect the better experience?
3. If they were worse, what systematic variable, if changed, would give the operation the greatest chance of improving the specific experience that fell short?

4. This important concept should be noted for future use. Suffice it to say that you will ask these questions as you test the dynamic, operating systems you ultimately create to help deliver the vision.

D. Complete the Leadership Team Exercise #2 - Values

Ask the group of leaders to anonymously submit three values they think should be a part of the company's values. Write all of them down on a white board or flip chart and make tally marks next to the ones that are submitted more than once. Be sure to include your own.

Remember, you must believe in the values that are chosen since you are ultimately responsible for the performance of the company. They must assist you with decision-making. In fact, it is the decision-making that is most important. Later, when your company or department is functioning problems will occur. They may be people problems, systems problems, results problems, or a myriad of other problems. Most of the problems will not have simple black and white solutions, but instead, will be in the gray. Very few things about running a business these days have easy black and white solutions.

When problems occur, you must, as the leader, refer to the values you selected and allow them to inform your decision-making. Then, take appropriate action consistent with what you, at the beginning of your journey, decided was non-negotiable for your company. If you allow problems to linger that are obviously in direct opposition to your stated values, you will lose credibility with your customers and team members, and anyone else who takes a hard look at your company.

If there are any that you have determined are non-negotiable, now would be a good time to let everyone know. As the results become obvious, let everyone know that, for the moment, you will hold the top 6–10 values submitted as place holders, pending the input received at the all-team meeting.

E. **Complete the Leadership Team Exercise #3 - LCP Process and Timeline Review**

Work together on a project management chart – a GANTT Chart is one option – showing the entire journey and the key milestones along the way. Include dates for key meetings such as:

- Executive Leadership Team Meetings
- All-Team Meetings
- Strategy Sessions
- Departmental Meetings

Also, estimate the dates specific objectives will be accomplished:

- A Company Vision Statement
- Core Values
- The Ideal Organizational Chart
- Updated written systems
- Additional training for teams where changes are occurring
- Initial measurement of new system impact
- Anything else you believe will be necessary.

F. **Conduct a Q&A until everything is out on the table**

At this point, you are starting to generate synergy with your executive leadership team. Hopefully, there is a sense of eager anticipation for the upcoming inclusion of your entire team, which will happen as we begin Phase 2 in Chapter 8. Well done.

Leadership Tool Box

- Company-wide work is a guide for departmental work.
- Master timelines are critical.
- Cliches to communicate needs
- Vision compared to actual operations

Chapter 8

APPLY THE TOOLS, PHASE 2 THE TEAM

Now that your company's team leaders are on board and the work has begun, it is time to include your subordinate leaders and front-line people in the process. Here is a more specific overview of the steps in using the LCP tool, Phase 2:

I. Rally the team at an all-team meeting.

  A. Rally support and share data
  B. Introduce the LCP process to the entire team
  C. Q & A
  D. Collect anonymous suggestions for vision and values
  E. Discuss "Mission to Systems" Clarity Tool
  F. Collect systems improvement suggestions

II. **Post all-team meeting results.**
   A. Create and post values and systems improvement suggestions
   B. Finalize the company's core values
   C. Create company's vision statement
   D. Distribute vision statement and values to all team members

Your first step towards achieving the goals of Phase 2 is an all-team meeting. If your company is too large for a company-wide meeting, you may choose to break the meeting up by department or take a couple of departments at a time. You can also meet virtually, but if you really want to make an impact on your company, bring everyone together at the same time.

Accomplish something incredible and unexpected, thereby clearly signaling to every team member that the status quo is over; and now is the time for the company to reach new heights in customer satisfaction, team-member satisfaction and, of course, bottom-line performance. In this make-or-break step, you will first let your people know where the company is now – and then why it needs to be better. You will also ask for each team member's anonymous opinions about values and vision and, as importantly, what the company can do to help them be incredibly successful with the task ahead.

As the leader of the team, there may be no other single action that you can do that will have a more lasting effect than the way you run the all-team meeting – so be prepared. If public speaking is not your strongest attribute, rehearse. Most importantly, be authentic. Also, be vulnerable yet strong – interested yet knowing – focused yet flexible – and subtly control the team-member input.

Remember to openly share positive energy with the group while enthusiastically recognizing team-member contributions. Conversely, invite any non-constructive, negative energy to be shared privately. Some criticism should come out in the meeting. In fact, from my experience, the meeting will more effectively enlist the team if some negative comments do come out. What matters is the intent of the negative or critical comment. Is the team member's intent to better the company for everyone? If yes, you have to let the comment be said. How you react will go a long way towards earning the team's respect. However, emotional and personal attacks are for behind closed doors. This is not the forum to air "dirty laundry."

I. Rally the Team at an All-Staff Meeting

A. Rally Support and share data

Thank everyone for attending and explain *why* such a big group has been brought together. Let everyone know that you have two goals:

- to improve the performance of the company in all areas, and
- to create a better quality of life for everyone.

Have fun and share your enthusiasm for this effort. Perhaps start the meeting by asking everyone on one side of the room to get up and find someone on the other side whom they have never met, and shake hands and introduce themselves.

Then appreciate and empower the team by recognizing someone from each department and single out their positive performance. Have them stand up while you speak about them. Be specific and detailed about what they did and how that type of performance will lead the company to greater levels of success.

Now, have some fun. Play a game. Here is a suggestion.

Play Company Trivia

- Ask fun questions and reward correct answers with movie tickets, gift cards or other prizes.
- For example: How many tees are in this jar? What are our company's gross sales each year? How many team members do we have? How do you make a hollandaise sauce? What planet did the movie "Avatar" take place on?

Be sure to have team members raise their hands to answer. I know from experience that everyone will yell out answers, which makes it tough to determine who answered first. Give the reward to the first person who can correctly answer – have fun with it.

Now you can transition into the business portion of the meeting.

- Show everyone the budget and relevant KPI for the current year then compare them to actual performance.
- Talk about what the competition is up to and how important it is to remain relevant to your customers.

- Discuss how company success means team-member success. If this has not been the case in the past, personally commit to it now.
- Tell them, "We need each one of you to join us in an incredible process. We can't do it without you. But, at the end of this presentation, if you don't think all this effort, positive energy and appreciation is for you, no problem. You can certainly opt out."

B. Introduce the LCP process to the entire team

Talk about what the leadership team has been doing to prepare for the LCP process and Introduce the **Leadership Clarity Pyramid.** Thoroughly cover the process each department will be following to achieve its goals and express its vision.

Discuss timelines, strategy and challenges. Mention the challenges of remaining relevant within your industry. Discuss the economy, competition and team-member quality of life. Show them the budget and performance numbers as they are now, and discuss goals for where they will be when the process has been completed. These can be financial or survey scores, or net promoter scores, or all of them.

Be honest about the new style of trust and communication that you are proposing – let them know that it will not always be comfortable – but is necessary to continuously improve. Take responsibility for any mediocrity that exists, but let them know those days are over. Now, ask for their help.

C. Q & A

While being sensitive to team-member input, you must also guide the process with your own experience and knowledge of what the company is going to need to be successful. Your company needs you to lead your team members to a conclusion that works. This does not mean to stifle their creativity – it means using your communication skills to create clarity about the true meaning of the comments made by your staff. They must know that you, and the leadership team:

1. Hear them
2. Care about what they say
3. Will back up the discussions with action
4. Will not penalize them for honest communication
5. Have a plan to make great things happen

6. Have the passion and integrity to make it great for everyone.

D. Collect anonymous suggestions for vision and values

Distribute paper and pens and ask for anonymous responses to the following questions:

1. "What should our company's values be in light of the things we've just talked about?"

Gently guide them by giving examples based on your management team's suggestions of what will be necessary for your company to thrive. Let them know "Continuous Improvement" has to be one of them. If you include continuous improvement as a core value, you will create another opportunity to tap directly into your most important asset – your people. Even if system improvements do not improve the bottom line immediately, how valuable is it to have every one of your employees actively and intelligently looking for ways to create a more efficient business? I say it is priceless. Not only are their brains turned on, but also they feel included in the process. They are not just punching a clock – they are active participants in your company's striving for success.

2. "What is your vision for your department or the company as a whole?"

Give them plenty of time to write. This can be a tough assignment for leaders, let alone, front-line team members. Let everyone know that you are not expecting polished vision statements, but would truly appreciate short statements of what their hopes are for their success and work environment.

E. Discuss the "Mission to Systems" Clarity Tool

Often leaders struggle to communicate the role of systems when creating clarity. An excellent teaching tool that helps team members understand the importance of systems was shared with me over 20 years ago by Bill Wernersback of Club Consulting – thank you, Bill! I have updated it a bit to make it as clear as possible. Visually share the following sequence and discuss as shown. Because systems are the means to communicate how your company and people will do what they do, this exercise bridges the gap between the more ethereal concepts of vision and mission and the solid clarity of systems. Plainly stated: Intangible (mission) to tangible (systems).

It starts like this, **"All companies have the same mission: Customer Satisfaction."**

The Mission – Customer Satisfaction
Satisfied customers pay their bill.

The Goal – A Positive Benefit-to-Cost Ratio
If the *Mission* is to produce satisfied customers, then the *Goal* is to produce a positive benefit-to-cost ratio. Simply put, the benefits outweigh the cost.

The Objective – Excellent Services and Experiences
If the *Goal* is to create a positive benefit to cost ratio, then the *Objective* is to provide excellent services and customer experiences to bolster the benefits side of the equation.

The Strategy – Enhance the Service and Experience Delivery Systems
If the *objective* is to provide excellent services and customer experiences, then the *Strategy* is to enhance the service and experience delivery systems that detail exactly how you deliver those excellent services and customer experiences.

Let your team know that you believe the quote from *Become Strategic or Die*: "No company can be as successful as possible unless every one of its team members is asking themselves every 30 minutes, 'Does it have to be done this way.' A team whose members have their brains turned on is an incredibly powerful force. Having said that, an excellent strategy is to ask your team members to, first, master the systems as they have been created.

I like to positively remind them of the many years of experience that went into their creation. Then, tell them that once they have mastered the systems, help the company make them better. Finally, I let team members know that this does not mean staying quiet if they have discovered a potentially damaging issue. I like to say, "If I am about to step in a hole and break my leg, please tell me." The same is true of your operations. If a team member honestly sees something that will break the company, they must not wait until it is too late to say something, whether they have mastered the current strategic systems or not.

F. Collect system improvement suggestions

This exercise sends a powerful signal to your team that they are crucially important to the success of the company. Ask them

- "Please give us your anonymous suggestions for system improvements that could make our company more effective. How can we do a better job of creating an environment for you to be incredibly successful?"

Give them as much time as needed to finish their comments, then collect them face down – no names are required. Be sure the team understands that all of their strategies, systems, and action plans will be evaluated by top-leadership prior to implementation to ensure consistency with any new vision and values statements. Also, be transparent. Let the team know that some suggestions may not be used and that is okay; and that you will post the suggestions in a conspicuous place with comments on whether the suggestion can be used or not, and if so, how and when.

Now might be a good time for the pizza and sodas to arrive. As the meeting moves to socializing and eating, sincerely let the team know how much you appreciate everyone's input and thank them again.

Before closing the meeting, thank everyone again and then provide a clear review of what is about to occur.

- Review what your leadership team will do post-meeting (covered in the next section)
- Review the expected timeline
- Let the team know that you and your leadership team will do your very best to move through this effort as effectively as possible – however, you fully anticipate that mistakes may be made
- Thank them, in advance, for their patience and reiterate that everyone is in this together
- Invite them to be a part of a very special time for everyone at the company.

II. Post all-team meeting results

As soon as possible after the all-team meeting, and as you have previously scheduled on your project management timeline, meet with your executive leadership to review the next steps for your leadership team. Once again, your ability to deliver results on a predetermined timeline will be an important signal to your teams that you can lead. Therefore, it is critical that you continuously check your project management tool to stay on schedule or, if necessary, make adjustments. Do not just fall behind and not address the issues that are causing the delays.

This portion of the process is crucially important. These are the first actions after the all-team meeting that you will take to prove to your entire team that you are serious about delivering what you have promised. You told everyone in your all-team meeting that you were going to do this. Now it is time to deliver.

A. Create and post values and system improvement suggestions

Write out the values suggestions – list the value and the number of times it was suggested, with the ones receiving the highest number of entries at the top. On a separate sheet, take all valid system suggestions and list them. Do not write duplicates. Simply list the ones that are unique. Format the spreadsheet so that it lists the suggestions by area, department, or concern. Remove any pointed negative remarks against specific individuals within the company. However, do not ignore these comments. If you sensed this situation before, or if you receive multiple comments regarding one person, you will need to address them – but not through the leadership clarity suggestions spreadsheet process.

For each suggestion, include a "status" and comments. The different "status" could be:

- Under review
- Done
- Great idea
- Not now
- Will review for next budget cycle

Every legitimate comment deserves a response to let the team member know that they are heard, but not every suggestion must receive an action.

Once completed, post the spreadsheet in a highly-visible area(s) to let team members review the issues, suggestions and progress. Be sure to remind them again and again how much you appreciate their engagement in the process.

B. Finalize company's core values

Due to the solid work already accomplished, you now have these resources available for this effort:

- The values that you, as the ultimate leader of your company believe are non-negotiable.
- The 6 - 10 values that were identified by your executive leadership team during their preparation for the LCP process.
- The all-team values suggestions rated by the frequency that they were mentioned.

In order to complete this task with values that are relevant to your team and serve the company well, you will want to reflect on the KPI that must be accomplished. You will also want to think through what you believe will best serve that effort while also creating a basis for team member satisfaction. Select six that you feel are best, and at the previously scheduled meeting to finalize your values, present them to your executive team for comment. After discussion, choose your final. It is highly recommended that at least one of the values be from the top of the all-team meeting suggestion list.

C. Create company's vision statement

The process of creating a vision statement can land anywhere from simple to incredibly complex. If you Google, "Vision Statements," you'll get 1.7 billion results. That is "1.7 billion" with a "b." Needless to say, vision statements are powerful tools for creating team clarity – and *Leadership Chaos to Clarity* is all about clarity. However, the topic of creating them is justification for so many books that I hesitate to venture too deeply into the subject. However, the following information should provide you with some solid perspective, and hopefully the ability to create something meaningful for your company.

Wikipedia describes vision statements as, "…an inspirational statement of an idealistic emotional future of a company or group. Vision describes the basic human emotion that a founder intends to be experienced by the people with whom the organization interacts."

Here are some examples of vision statements that are considered to be amongst the best:

- Nordstrom – To serve our customers better, to always be relevant in their lives, and to form lifelong relationships.
- IKEA – To create a better everyday life for the many people.
- Disney – To be one of the world's leading producers and providers of entertainment and information.

- Southwest Airlines – To be the world's most loved, most efficient, and most profitable airline.

As you brainstorm your company's vision statement try to combine what is important to three constituencies: your customers, your team members and the company.

According to Michael Keenan at Starting Up writing for Shopify in March of 2022:

- "A vision statement is an aspirational statement made by a company that outlines long-term goals. A successful vision statement inspires employees and steers an organization's efforts."
- "Behavioral statistician Joseph Folkman performed a research study on vision statements and how they can affect a business's success. His 2014 study found that employees who think their organization's vision is meaningful show positive engagement levels 52% higher than if they didn't."
- "What that means is an inspiring vision statement causes employees to be invested in your company's journey toward achieving your desired plans. Inspired employees inspire

customers, and that passion will make your vision a reality."
- "A vision statement provides a brief description of a company's long-term goals. It's typically ambitious and communicates how the company plans to make a difference in the world. Think of it as a roadmap for making decisions that align with your company's philosophy and objectives."

As you begin to create yours keep these suggestions in mind:

- Keep it short. If you write a book for your vision statement, it is quite likely no one will read or remember it, particularly your team members – and its impact will be greatly reduced or completely lost.
- Align your vision statement with the work you have already accomplished as a part of the LCP process. For example: your vision, values, strategies, goals and KPI.

At Trophy Club Country Club, we changed our approach and focused instead on the impact that a vision statement could have on the way team members think about their jobs, and what is necessary for them to deliver quality member or guest experiences. The belief was that if team members could simply be in alignment and committed to our vision, the rest would take care of itself. With that in mind, we created this vision statement: "TCCC is a company where every team member owns their zone for it being neat, clean, organized and operationally effective."

D. Distribute vision statement and core values to all team members

Now that the values and vision statement are completed, use several means to share the chosen values and vision statement with the entire team – post flyers, send an email, create and distribute business cards with the vision and values on them.

Before moving on, has anyone opted out of all this? Have you encountered managers in your company that you know are not able to make it happen? Let us be real – the longer you allow them to remain in your organization, the longer it will take for great things to begin happening. As great leaders understand, sometimes a company needs to let everyone in the organization know that you mean business. That may mean letting popular managers move on. Please do not take this the wrong way. Most often, this only occurs after you have coached and counseled until you are "blue in the face" trying to persuade the team member to be a part of the company's excellence initiative.

Once you have reached that point, you can be assured that everyone in the company knows what is going on; and if you do not let them go, you will undermine your reputation as a leader who will do whatever is necessary to accomplish the company's goals.

Now, refer to the project-management chart and let everyone know your timelines for creating new strategies and systems for each department. In the next chapter you will get "real" with your leadership team and discover evidence of shortfalls and weaknesses in their systems; and, as importantly, you will determine the potential financial and other impacts of a proper solution. The new strategies and systems created from those strategies are the most important means to deliver improved KPI results.

Leadership Tool Box

- Vision Statement
- The Clarity Tool: All companies have the same mission.

Chapter 9

DYNAMIC SYSTEM IMPLEMENTATION

When a business refuses to seek and embrace change, its people burn out. They object to what they are asked to do and complain about the performance of management.

—BECOME STRATEGIC OR DIE

At this point in the use of the LCP you and your leadership team have accomplished a great deal. However, it is the next steps that will determine the long-term effectiveness of your efforts. Those steps include the creation and implementation of written, strategically-improved operating systems.

So far you have conducted your all-team meeting and come away with:

- Suggestions for company vision and values
- Suggestions for how to help team members be incredibly successful
- A team ready for the next steps.

Department Head Team Assignment #1: Implement LCP Tools in their areas

Now that your team leaders know what to do, assign them the following tasks:

1. Evaluate the current performance of their departments.
   a. Financials vs. Budget, Financials vs. Forecast, Financials vs. Goals
   b. Customer satisfaction vs. Goals
   c. Employee satisfaction vs. Goals
   d. Product delivery vs. Vision
   e. Cultural environment vs. Values
2. Review the values and systems improvement suggestions garnered from the all-team meeting that are relevant to their operations.
3. Create a timeline for LCP Tools implementation.

To get started, identify the areas in your company that, if improved, would have the greatest positive impact on customer satisfaction, team-member clarity, or the achievement of financial goals. Pre-meeting, assign team members who will be attending the strategy sessions the task of answering the question, "How can the company help you be incredibly successful at your job?"

Schedule strategy sessions with all team members required to cover relevant topics. Let them know upfront that the sessions may include constructive conflict. Such conflict, while absolutely necessary to achieve the best results, may be uncomfortable. Additionally, attendees must be told that the goal is to discover the best-possible solutions, and therefore, some good ideas will not be used. Assure everyone that there are no bad ideas. Any idea not chosen as the final solution will be kept in reserve should the strategy chosen not deliver the results required.

1. Collect and distribute for pre-session review every current operating system that governs *how* and *what* that area of your company does.
2. Execute and record the sessions, either with a scribe or video. Once complete, distribute the recordings to all participants.

3. Assign team leaders the task of translating the session into strategic *actions* they will take to improve their operating systems and therefore, their operational results.
4. Review the actions suggested for their probability to deliver required results. If approved, change the systems and add measurement tools.
5. Distribute all changes and train all team members.
6. Ensure all new performance is congruent with new strategies.
7. Measure the success of the changes.
8. Repeat with other departments.

Whenever possible, the strategy sessions should include the stakeholders who will be responsible for operating the systems that are ultimately created. When you include subordinate leaders and, if appropriate, frontline team members, in the process you save time and reduce future pain because any decisions that you document in your systems should include the insights of those who will be governed by them.

Additionally, commit yourself and the company to have whatever level of talent is necessary for the sessions to produce world-class results. If the talent to create new systems that will achieve your vision and the necessary financial results does not exist in your company, who might you add to the sessions? From experience, you cannot casually gather your current team members in a room, ask them to think outside the box, and suddenly create radically improved financial results. This is bound to be tough sledding. Additionally, the leader must expect to push for world-class ideas. That means probing and prodding participants until they share what is really on their mind. Consider using a meeting facilitator so that you, as the leader, can focus more on contributing to the discussion and potential new strategies.

For these sessions to have the greatest possible chance to be successful, you must:

- Be thoroughly prepared
- Have the proper facility
- Include the correct team members, consultants or facilitators
- Have copious amounts of data

- Create an environment that nurtures creativity, trust and transparency
- Limit interruptions and turn off cell phones

In addition, introducing something unconventional will both relax your team and signal to them that you are willing to do whatever it takes to succeed. So, consider doing some improv, listen to some music, meditate or try some trust exercises. All of these efforts are meant to assist you in creating a fertile environment for maximum productivity.

Once agreed upon, mandate that first-draft updates of operating systems be completed and provide a deadline. Inspect the drafted operations manual updates to ensure that they accurately communicate the desired actions.

As you work through the strategy step, whether at the top of the organization or departmentally, it is critical to document all ideas in an organized fashion so they can be easily interpreted to create **written, dynamic operating systems** (step 4 of the LCP).

Your new strategically updated systems will be used to communicate how operations will work going forward, and must also include the following:

- Tools that measure if the strategic changes are implemented correctly.
- Tools that measure if the changes produce the required results.

Be sure to address and answer these needs in your strategy sessions or you will find yourself repeating the process.

First Draft Updated Operations Manuals

Assign the task of creating first-draft implementation action plans. Ideas for change mean nothing if not implemented with a detailed plan.

Inspect all plans for timeline, context, constraints, budgets, training requirements, systems changes, marketing the change in-house, and sharing the reasons for change with front-line team members. Remind your leaders that they must use the quality input and suggestions from the all-team meeting to complement the system modifications that are in draft form.

As you or your department heads write the operations manuals, leave as little to individual discretion as possible. Team members will be required to use their own judgment in unforeseeable circumstances. However the more performance areas are standardized, the greater the predictability of overall company performance.

As a leader, you cannot create an environment for transparent accountability unless the accountability measures are clearly written and communicated to everyone. Accountability then becomes a standard operating procedure, and the penalty for non-performance is clearly understood by all persons who call themselves "team members."

All changes require measurement tools that will test any suggestion for actual improvement. If no measurable improvement occurs, alternative plans must be implemented. Do not allow ineffective system changes to remain in place. This leadership clarity effort demands that the most effective processes are found and put in place; if the modifications are not producing the financial and customer-satisfaction results necessary to sustain your vision for your company, the LCP process should be repeated.

When your team leaders have received and reviewed action plans that will potentially change an operating system in their department, they must change the master operations manuals and distribute the revisions.

While it may seem simple, modifying systems and, ultimately, team-member behavior is anything but simple. Systems changes can be the hardest for team members because of the following:

- Team members will be asked to change their normal behavior.
- A greater level of accountability may appear to be present in their department, and they may resent being singled out.
- Team members may not initially agree with the system change. Many times, changes are hard at first and, initially, do not produce performance improvements. Only after mastering the changes and consistently performing them as instructed do team members normally begin to see the benefits.
- The new plan may create more challenging work for some team members without them receiving an increase in compensation.

A good way to reduce the stress that system change, or improvement, may have on current team members is to be completely prepared. Accomplish the following prior to taking the new system to the team:

1. Let the departmental team members know, ahead of time, that an action-plan team is working on an issue within their department.
2. Before a system modification is completely accepted, test it to see if it "holds water" in practice. Allow affected team members to try it, and then comment on possible modifications or shortcomings. These comments may act as a final test of the system improvement.
3. Once the processes are proven to have a strong chance at creating something positive, make it a permanent part of the departmental operations manuals, and begin measuring its effectiveness over an appropriate amount of time.

   - Update your departmental master operations manuals
   - Modify the job descriptions and checklists that are governed by the master operations manual
   - Distribute updated materials to appropriate team members

- Implement the new standard and begin the use of a modified performance measurement tool

Early in the new system implementation, management must closely monitor individual team-member performance to ensure that new behaviors are implemented exactly as planned. If team members get sloppy in their execution, there will be no way of knowing if measured results were the result of the updated system or the inconsistent performance of the team members acting under the system.

Leadership Tool Box

- Are changes implemented correctly?
- Are changes producing desired results?

Chapter 10

SUCCESS

Your operations will never be perfect. Your implementation of the LCP process will also not be perfect. You can, however, be open, honest and vulnerable. Admit to your team upfront that you are not perfect and acknowledge that some level of imperfection will come from them as well. Having said that, what level of imperfection is acceptable?

Here is how I explain it: I call it the 95% or better approach. I, personally, will aim to deliver 100% or better at all times. This is my personality. It justifies, in my mind, why I can hold all others accountable. Team Members are expected to deliver a minimum of 95% or better. I really want 98% but will accept 95+%. Why would I accept this? Because people get sick. Their pets get hit by cars. Their kids get in trouble. Their cars break down. If you keep demanding 100% and then stress about everyone's inability to deliver at that level, and you will quickly lose the trust of those you need most.

Why is 95% a number to work with? I use the example of scientists in a lab mixing two test tubes of content, an agent and reagent. If they can mix them and achieve the same result 95% or better of the time, it is considered a valid result. I think the same is true with business operations. If you are shocked that I would work with this approach and before you send me a letter telling me I am crazy, try to name a few companies that get it right every time. There are not any. They may correct their mistakes really well – but get it right the first time, every time? None.

So now, when I speak to team members, I have a legitimate rallying call - 95% or better! They get it and can buy in.

There are, in fact, certain leadership characteristics that, if present, will greatly improve the level of success you can expect from this program. These highly desirable characteristics are:

- Leadership that believes in the power of rigorous teamwork and is willing to set the example
- Leadership that understands the need to, and has the willingness to embrace change and continuous improvement in order to remain relevant to consumers and inspire team members
- Leadership that has a willingness to dedicate time to this process
- Leadership that understands and is willing to accept that doing what is necessary to achieve success may initially require increased work hours, before opening the pathway to achieve a positive work and life balance
- Leadership that is dedicated to doing whatever is necessary to ensure success, even if it is initially uncomfortable.

Accountability will be crucial during the early stages of a new system rollout. Your team will be watching to see if leadership is, indeed, committed to the rigorous standards, goals and culture that the new systems dictate. If you or any of your leadership team members fail to vigorously inspect the day-to-day operations and ensure that they fully represent the new systems, your efforts will fail. If you fail to measure the new financial results and customer-satisfaction scores that result since the implementation of the **Leadership Clarity Pyramid**, your efforts will fail.

Simply stated, if you have no intention to, or are unable to follow through with the necessary accountability, you may as well not have begun. The team members will quickly lose faith, not only in the **LCP** process, but also in the leadership team who has promised clarity and delivered something far less.

Additionally, be keenly aware that you will have difficult personnel decisions to make. What company does not? The difference here is that this program will require you to make them, or risk losing the confidence of your entire team. If, during this process, you determine that you have "gray area" performers who will not respond to the leadership clarity effort and, at the same time you are demanding 95+% effort from everyone else, you have to address them or no one else will believe that you have committed the company to achieve its finest-possible performance. As I like to say,

"Don't hold average performers back from their future careers...with someone else."

Timing

As you prepare for this exciting program, give some thought to the timing. Is the timing right for this type of effort? If your company is just entering its busiest season, now might not be the best time to begin an initiative like this one. Perhaps working through your high season while taking copious notes on your company's performance will make you more aware of the challenges that this program may rectify.

Before we leave this topic, busy season or not, if your company is falling apart, or is in dire need of a metamorphosis, "you've got to do what you have to do" – *so get started as soon as you can!*

One final thing to consider before you begin: do you need outside assistance to ensure that your company will invest the kind of effort necessary to complete the **LCP** process? Many leaders are so tied up in the day-to-day business of the business (working "in" the business), that they cannot make the time for this type of effort, (working "on" the business). If this is the case with you, maybe an outside consultant should be hired to facilitate your company's efforts.

In closing, I would like to leave you with some of the outstanding and life-changing books that have added to my collective leadership consciousness. Here are some of the books that made a difference:

The E-Myth Revisited by Michael Gerber. Systems. Organizational chart exercise. Attention to detail.

Ethics for the New Millenia by His Holiness, the Dalai Lama. Two things human beings have in common – the desire to reduce suffering and the desire to increase happiness. Have you ever considered these as you create systems that govern what and how your people do what they do?

The Seven Habits of Highly Effective People by Stephen Covey. I was lucky enough to work at the Washington Athletic Club (WAC) when Jim Johnson was the general manager. He had worked with Stephen Covey and made *Seven Habits* required reading for all leadership teams at the WAC. I thank Jim for doing this; and I sincerely thank Mr. Covey for having written such an impactful and important book.

Let's Get Real or Let's Not Play by Mahan Khalsa. Clarity! How to focus on helping potential clients be successful, rather than try to sell them on anything. His examples using red, yellow and green lights in the sales process are so simple and yet, so important.

Good to Great by Jim Collins. While general manager at the venerable Indianapolis Athletic Club, Eli Lilly was providing this book to its leaders. If it is good enough for Eli Lilly, it is good enough for me. Brilliant in so many areas. Share it with your team and talk about the implications of all portions of it for your company.

The Five Dysfunctions of a Team by Pat Lencioni. I read about the book in *USA Today*. Apparently, NFL coaches were using it; so I thought it would be worth the read. Wow. It was so important that I bought the facilitators book and materials and have used it over and over. It literally has changed the trajectory of companies for the better. All else being equal, teamwork is the ultimate competitive advantage. Can you lead a group to achieve it?

The Three Signs of a Miserable Job by Pat Lencioni. So straightforward. Check it out. Are they known? Can they measure their own performance? Do they know how their performance affects all others?

Of course, there are many other books that I have read, but these helped me to mature as a leader. And after many years of performing in the field, I have created my own original thoughts and formed my **LCP** process. Use it and it will change your leadership life for the better. More importantly, it will help you teach the leaders who report to you how to make great things happen for their team.

Remember, leadership's job is to create an environment for their teams to be incredibly successful. I trust that *Leadership Chaos to Clarity* has shown you how to do that and how to implement the strategy quickly. You now have the opportunity to change peoples' lives – including yours – for the better. Do not forget, however, that while it is not rocket science, that does not mean it is easy.

Leadership Tool Box

- Your efforts will not be perfect.
- 95% or Better Communication to Team Members

Acknowledgements

With deep appreciation I acknowledge the support and guidance of the following people who have helped me grow as a person, entrepreneur, and leader, making this book possible.

Special thanks to the following mentors and educators that invested in me: Mrs. Carter, Mr. Raal, Dr. Mikeski, Dean Kellum.

My best wishes to great mentors, partners, and team members: Jim Johnson, Jerry Jones, Lisa Dawes, David Waldman, George Lidicker, Chuck Brownfield, Deborah Waldvogel, John Findley, Jason Becker, Lynn Josephson, Dylan Smith, Phil Romano, Keith Siergiej, Bill Wernersback, the entire TCCC Executive Leadership Team, Frank Merkel, and Rowan Samuel. A special thank you to my brother, Michael, for believing in me and helping with early edits.

Sincere thanks and appreciation to my world-class publishing team: April O'Leary, Publisher; Heather Desrocher, Editor; Kat Langenheim, Proofreader; Dustin Herl, Web Developer. When it comes to making "Vision" a reality you are the best.

Finally, much love to my wife, Amanda, my three boys, and my parents for their unflinching support and unconditional love.

About the Author

Tim Rowe has over 40 years of experience in the private club, hospitality, wellness and resort development fields. Most recently he was general manager at the vibrant Trophy Club Country Club in Trophy Club, Texas. He was also general manager of the Indianapolis Athletic Club, which was twice named as a "Platinum Club of America" during his tenure, and Pelican Isle Yacht Club in Naples, Florida.

His entrepreneurial background includes ownership and operational leadership in T. Emerson Rowe – Hospitality and Club Consulting, Sedona Resorts Management as Director of Operations, The Fitness Source, Inc., and Golf Life Navigators (GLN). Tim has been married to his wife, Amanda, for over 30 years. They have three wonderful boys. His hobbies include tennis, fitness, good wine, movies, music and travel. For more about Tim's work visit **timroweconsulting.com**.

www.ingramcontent.com/pod-product-compliance
Lightning Source LLC
Chambersburg PA
CBHW041325110526
44592CB00021B/2820